The B Principle,

The Strategy before the Strategy

By

Bruno Alvarez

The Accident and the aha moment

After working for a major global fuels company in Guatemala for six years, I found myself beginning a new job at a US owned, locally operated power generation company. Most global companies come down to Latin American countries to set themselves on an adventure of expanding their business to reach countries with a lot of challenges. The major hurdles are the governments and industries filled with corruption. After some time, they sell and leave the country. That's what happened to my previous employer, the fuels company. After some safety incidents and local government bribery attempts, they decided that being in these markets was in detriment to the value of the brand. They sold their assets to a company based in Honduras.

I moved to work for an American power generation company who had stake in several countries in Latin America. I´m a chemical engineer who specializes in supply chain, specifically procurement and strategic sourcing. I was contracting major capital expense projects for several fuels' depot and service stations. In my new role I had to source fossil fuels and mineral coal for the power plants and finish the sourcing of a new coal plant, something very novel in Guatemala since there were but a few in all Central America.

My new boss left the company on my first day that I reported to work. So it happens that a few months later there was a major bust by US federal agencies because a group of directors stole some eighteen million dollars in a triangular scheme in the purchase of the new coal plant. No wonder my original boss fled the country earlier. Anyway, I was left with no reporting line. I came into this job referred to by the local purchasing manager with whom I worked with before. Suddenly he was left in charge, and I had a dotted line to him and a dotted line to a manager in Charlotte who knew nothing from the international business.

The Coal plant was late and over budget. I was charged with the duty of expediting and basically fixing the sourcing part of the project. Our local supply chain was made up of basically junior buyers and I was the only strategic sourcing person. I had to take care of the heavy load. Our office was set in a corporate building uptown Guatemala. All nice marble and glass and very corporate. But every Friday I travel some 60 miles into the coastline to the new plant site.

I will travel with the project manager to a half day meeting with the contractors and engineering team. We leave early in the morning to be there at eight am sharp. The project manager, a very seasoned engineer that had done a lot of similar projects and his assistant. A local lady in her late twenties married with two young children all full of energy. The rest of the day we will have individual meetings with the team and run by the plant under construction to see some details and understand some of the issues to resolve. It was a very intense trip, and it was also fun at the same time. You will get contagious of the adrenaline on the field and the passion of the engineers. Overall, to me it was fun although at the end of the day I was bushed.

One of the buyers from my team was the one who was more experienced. When rumors came that there was going to be a position of more seniority, he asked to participate in the recruitment process. He had a lot of experience in the mechanics field and knew a lot about purchasing for the other power plants. Everybody had high expectations on him being the one for this role. When I came along and got the role he was devastated. He was mad and really started to despise the company. His anger and frustration led him to look for work in another company. So, it happens he landed a job in another power company. We worked together for a while and became good coworkers, no grudges there.

The day he resigned the whole purchasing team decided to give him a farewell party. The following Friday everyone got into two cars and drove to a beach that was near the power plant to spend the weekend. I was going to join them after the Friday routine project meeting with the project manager assistant. Since I was new to the team and the organization, I was in search of work and sometimes some processes take time. Usually, you try more than one lead in your job hunt and in my case one of these leads came knocking at my door after I accepted in the power company. It was a major cement company. They said that the role was delayed but they wanted me to continue a process I thought was a dead end. Unexpectedly, I was called to an assessment panel on Saturday, on the same weekend as the farewell party. I decided to go to the assessment panel.

Friday afternoon I went to a restaurant halfway to the beach house and took the project manager assistant to meet with the purchasing team so she can switch cars and go with them. I headed back to the city to get a good night sleep and be prepared for an early assessment panel process the next day. It was an awful experience. There was this girl that had the right answers to everything the panel asked. I knew I was the best fitted for the role, but she was all over with her answers. I knew I flunked and at noon it all ended. I knew it was not going to happen. Still, I was sad but ok since I already was working, I still had a new job.

Around three pm I received a call that Saturday. It was about the time the purchasing team was going to head back from the beach. I kind of sensed it was them. I was correct, one of the younger buyers, a girl that is very smart and energetic called. I said how are you? All good! She answers with a very weary voice. No, we are not ok! We are not ok at all! We had a car accident! The car flipped many times. I'm sitting in the car trapped and the people riding in the back are missing.

The guy that was leaving the team was driving this girl's car, a Peugeot 206 that she just purchased a couple of weeks before. She was riding in the passenger seat. In the back there where two girls. One was a seasoned buyer who had worked for the company for some ten years or so. She started as an assistant and later became a buyer. The other girl was the project manager assistant. The driver and passenger were using their seat belts as expected. The two girls in the back had no seat belt. Odd to say because in this company safety was of the utmost importance due to the line of business, power generation with fuels. We had all sorts of training and protocols to comply with safety, including safe driving. I still don´t understand why they were not using the seat belt in the back. We always did. We would drive to the plant frequently with all safe driving measures.

It is not clear what happened exactly, but they were going above speed limit when for some reason the driver did a sharp turn, probably avoiding hitting something. The car flipped several times, the driver's arm got out the window and scrapped the floor several times. The two girls in the back got tossed out the car and flew several feet away. One landed on the asphalt and the other on the side of the road on some grass. The passenger who was the one that called me described the scene as she called when the car stopped flipping. She said that the driver was screaming in pain because his arm was destroyed. She managed to get out of the car through the window and walked to the other girls. The one that landed on the asphalt had trouble breathing and as she described to me what she saw; she gave away her last breath. She started looking for the other girl and could not reach her. The grass was really tall, and the ground was very irregular. She was still alive but unconscious. I asked her if there was anyone nearby. She said there were a couple of people from a nearby village. They had called an ambulance and it would reach them in about twenty minutes since it was far from the crash site. I got cut off. In that instance I started calling as many people as I could that could help. First, I called the plant manager. I knew he was at the plant, and it was near. He quickly moved and reached the site fast. I also called my boss who called the human resources manager. The word got out quickly and the whole organization got moving. At the plant we had an in-house medical team. They went to the hospital where the injured got moved. I got in the car and rushed to the plant.

When I got to the plant, they had the passenger at the plant and the other 3 injured at the hospital. Sad to say the project manager assistant died in the ambulance. She left a grieving husband and two small children. The other girl riding in the back had severe brain damage. She could never work again and needed assistance for the basic everyday tasks. The driver's arm was destroyed to the bone. He was moved to another hospital where he stayed for several months and underwent several surgeries in an effort to reconstruct his arm. He never recovered and lost all movement in his arm. The girl in the passenger seat was ok. A little bruised but ok. I drove her back to her house and told her father what had happened.

All this happened on Saturday and Sunday. The next Monday when I came to the office in the morning it was sad. Grieving people all over. Truly a down moment in my life and all in that knew the team. That Afternoon was the funeral of the project manager assistant. We closed the doors, and all went to the funeral. I had never been so sad and shocked in my life, and I could never forget how that moment went. We all cried and hugged each other. The next day was still surreal. We went to the office all numbed and to be honest little work was done. All the directors were in meetings, and everyone was trying to sort out what happened and why. At the end of the day, I was called into my boss office for a meeting. Just the two of us.

When the day was over and it got dark, I came into my boss office. We worked in a nice building, and he had a nice office with a view. The sunset was breathtaking. We went over what happened briefly and kind of grieved a little again. Then he started going into reality mode with the conversation. Basically, his purchasing team was diminished and all he had was the buyer girl who will come back in a day or two and me, the strategic guy to cover for all the department. I thought to myself, ok you can do this, let's try and solve this. He said how are we going to do this? I said Well we need a strategy. First let´s asses what is pending. We opened the requisition´s in our purchasing software and there were sixteen-hundred-line items to be purchased. For the complete purchasing team is something that is buyable. For just us two it was titanic. I said: you know we should do what we did in our old job at the fuels company. Remember? He answers: Actually, I do not remember. That was a very unexpected answer to be frank. Well, the purchasing team strived to be efficient. Fast at the purchase especially of the low spend items, and effective with the big spend items. Be fast with the bulk and spend time only with the big spend where it was worth it. He was impressed and happy to see there was a way forward after all. Me I had sort of an "aha" moment there.

I realized that purchasing follows the 80/20 rule where big spend was 20% of all transactions but 80% of all spend and small stuff was 80% transactions and 20% spend. But the "aha" moment came when I realized that the strategy for big spending was very different in nature that the one for the small spend. That was amazing to me. It was all spent but it was so different in the purchasing strategy. Two of a kind. This is what I decided to investigate and understand better. This principle as a corollary of the 80/20 rule was amazing for developing a strategy. This realization I decided to call the B principle and started to explore if it was true for purchasing does it apply to all cases of the 80/20 rule.

In the following chapters I will discuss first the science behind the B principle and how it applies to other functions in business and even in life. At the end I want to come back to what happened after the accident and some fishy things I found out that happened with my assessment, and the people involved in the hiring process. It is an unexpected twist of events, a story of deceit, and probably also prevented me from being in the accident that day.

The B principle explained.

In 1848 in Italy a very smart and sharp individual was born named Vilfredo Federico Damaso Pareto. He was a total academic and contributed as a civil engineer, sociologist, economist, political scientist, and philosopher. Some of his achievements, or for what he is most recognized, are in economics, in the study of income distribution and in the analysis of individuals´ choices. He also popularized the use of the term "elite" in social analysis. His legacy as an economist is profound. Before him the field of economy was more in line of a branch of moral philosophy as practiced by Adam Smith. He was more of a data scientist, intensive in the field of scientific research and mathematical logic. He was a great observer of nature and the natural patterns. He would apply his observations to develop the field of microeconomics.

One of the most remarkable observations made by Vilfredo Pareto was on how wealth was distributed in Italy. 80% of the wealth in Italy belonged to about 20% of the population. After this and other observations he realized that this relationship was present in many other cases. It was true in healthcare where 20% of patients incurred 80% of healthcare expenses. In manufacturing 80% of volumes incurred in 20% of product types. In Sales 80% sales come from 20% of clients, and so on. This became what we will call today the pareto principle also known as the 80/20 rule or the law of the vital few. In essence it states that:

For many outcomes, roughly 80% of the consequences comes from 20% of the causes (the vital few)

For me it came in the realization that in the purchasing department 80% of line items purchased were 20% of the total spend. The other 80% of the spend will come from the purchase of 20% of the line items. This will be what is called "the vital few". This represents the core of your data set. For me it was those line items that I had to carefully track spend. The bacon on my breakfast plate. Right after I realized this, I noticed something. This Vital Few I had to watch closely and negotiate well. But I could not undermine the other. They were as important because if it was not sourced fast, it might stop the operation incurring in losses. What I realized was that the strategy I had to follow for the top 20% or the vital few was very different from the other 80%. This is the core of the **B PRINCIPLE:**

For many outcomes, roughly 80% of the consequences come from 20% of the causes (the vital few) and the strategy for the vital few or top 20% is different in nature from the bottom 80%; two separate strategies should be considered for the total set.

In my case I developed two strategies based on my two sets of purchasing lines, the top spends items or what we called the vital few and the small spend items. For the big spend items I had to be Effective and bring in benefits from a good negotiation. For the low spend I needed to be Fast and accurate I had to be Efficient. I developed a graphics representation of the B Principle applied to my purchasing and contracting function (Diagram 1).

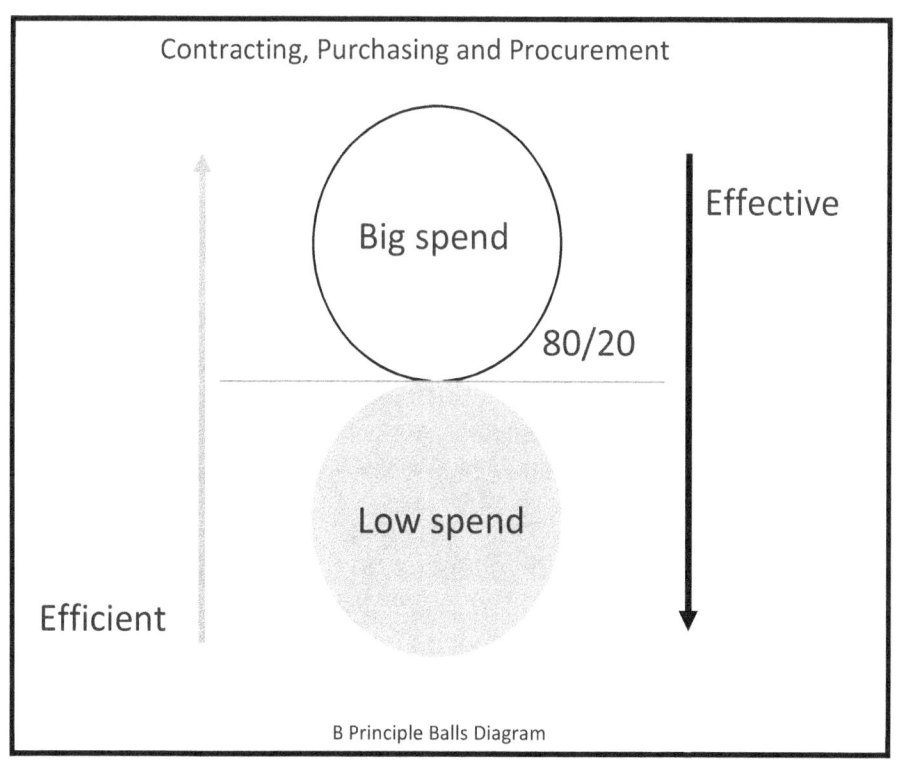

The Universe of consequences as stated in the Pareto Principle in this case will be the purchase line items. They are divided into two balls or universes. The big spend the top ball and the low spend the bottom ball. They are separated by a red line that indicates the top 20% big spend items and the 80% low spend Items. Then there is a vertical arrow. The one for the low spend goes from bottom to top and indicates in one word the strategy to follow "efficiently". For the top Spend that runs in importance from the highest spend down to the lowest it will be "effective" in the negotiations to bring savings and good terms and conditions. As you can see Efficient and effective are very different in nature and they convey very different actions. If you want to be efficient you will focus more on purchasing line items fast and getting them delivered fast, if you are going to be effective you will focus on the cost and terms of the purchase rather than moving fast and expediting the purchase.

The B principle can be applied as a corollary to the pareto principle and it follows along the law as a parallel. We can call it the strategy definition principle that follows the pareto principle. If the pareto principle occurs the B principle can be applied. As a visual description of the B principle the B principle balls diagram can be applied. In the following chapters the aim will be to challenge the B principle where the pareto principle applies, especially in business administration and finance. A similar diagram will be drawn to explain each example and hopefully teach how to use it as a template or aid to help develop the strategy set of two for each occurrence where the pareto principle is confirmed. The examples that will be used are confirmed cases where the pareto principle is confirmed from an extensive set of data observations and analysis. We will not venture to find new pareto principle occurrences but subscribe to the ones proven by facts.

Some examples where the pareto principle is observed are in warehouse inventories with a lot of items. If you focus on the top 20% of high value items, you can control 80% of the total value of the warehouse. Items can even be categorized according to value so you can identify the top 20% value. Categorization techniques can be applied such as ABC warehouse categorization. The A being the top value and B and C the lower value items.

Another example of the pareto principle being used and taken advantage of is in quality control of manufacturing goods. You can sample the top 20% of value items and have 80% of the total quality assessed, this will help focus efforts and help to define a good sample that represents the whole lot of total items.

Even in software development and debugging. Engineers can work on the top 20% tickets of errors and such and fix 80% of bugs and corrections to a software solution. It's everywhere, in business the top 20% of processes of the value chain represent 80% of the value of the total chain.

We shall explore some cases where the pareto principle is proven to be present. We shall then apply the B principle in the most common or best practice strategy used in that case. The aim is to display the practical use of the B principle more than the strategy used. The definition of the strategy can vary from case to case and should follow a case-by-case solution. The B principle is a guide to understand the duality of strategies needed for a set of causes to obtain the desired or best consequences. That's why we are not stating a strategy development process rather is the strategy before defining the strategy, or actually the two strategies that are needed for a pareto principle occurrence. To make it interest it will be displayed in the story form of case analysis so we can identify with real life cases and be also entertained in a storytelling type of narrative.

The B Principle in Sales

Sales is by far the tip of the arrow for most business. Since the industrial revolution the main attention has being given to the sales of goods and services. The most basic approach to business administration and the concept of being successful in a business is having good sales. Even the most rudimental business focus on sales and tracking them. On more modern times we look at other key performance indicators (KPI) but since the crack of times sales have been the most sought-after metric. How many sheep did you sell. The number of beers served; how many pounds of potatoes sold on the day at the market. If you sold a lot, you are good, if you sold little you have problems, as simple as that. As time passed sales have been handled in a more mature and predictive way. The core of today's data science is very well applied today to create predictive sales models and artificial intelligence algorithms to give state-of-the-art analysis, predictions, and business decisions on sales data.

But going back to the beginning Pareto studied the wealth spread of the population and within that study he noticed that his Pareto Principle applied to sales. The man who sold spices on the market had a few clients, roughly 20% of them, who would buy a lot and in a very constant weekly and biweekly way, about 80% of total sales. The rest will be sold once to a lot of clients, some of them, he will not see again in the year. The Pareto Principle will be true in sales. It is everywhere from shoes to food in the supermarket to online stores. It doesn't matter if it is a small store in a small town or a megastore in the center of a busy large city. It does not matter if it is low-cost goods or high-end products. The Pareto principle has a strong presence in all sales data analysis.

Going back to our example of the spice merchant in the market, as you may be thinking the B PRINCIPLE will apply? And how? Well, it is interesting that the top 80% sales come from a few, 20% of customers. This is where the name "vital Few" was coined to this select group. If you care about your sales, you take good care of your "vital Few". This is why your strategy is to have "happy customers". How? Well, you keep the products they need, understand their needs, and wants, free samples, delivery, extended warranty, special discounts, anything to keep them happy and return to make up the main core of your business. That will be the strategy 1 for the main customers. For the bottom customers the strategy will be efficient sales, prepacked one ounce bags, easy payment, no hassle purchases. This will be strategy 2. Let's see how this looks on the B PRINCIPLE balls diagram (Diagram 3).

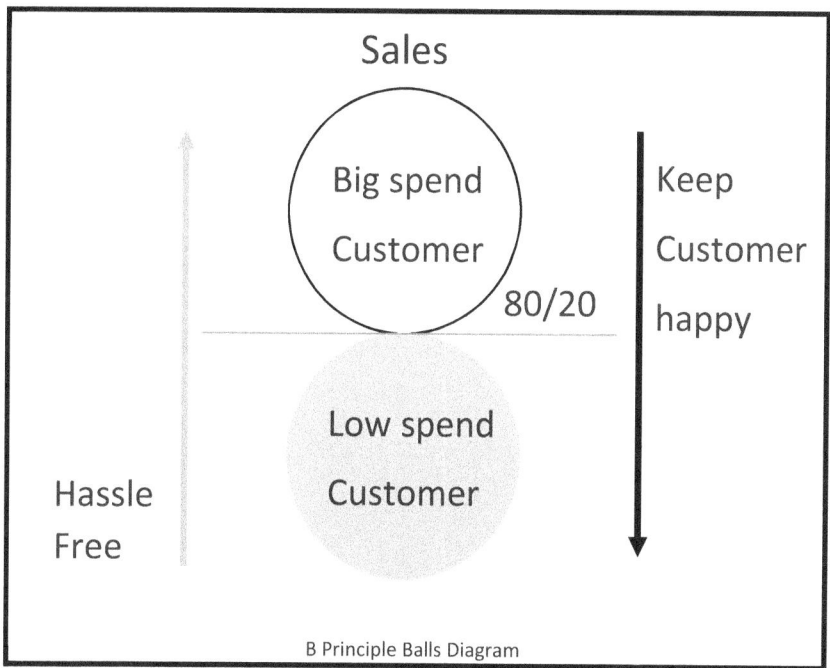

B Principle Balls Diagram

A very smart move in sales will be to try and move your low spend customers to become big spend customers. This would not be for all of them, but there is an opportunity to increase the size of your total spend in a sustainable way. Also, it is of great value to have identified the big spend customers and invest in keeping them happy. Sometimes when there is only one strategy there is a tendency to try and have happy customers overall. It is not a bad strategy, but you may stumble into trying to please and inverting a lot of energy on low spend customers and depleting your resources having nothing left for the big spend ones that matter more. Also, a low spend customer will certainly appreciate the hassle free experience since for him the purchase of low value is also his bottom 80% of matters of concern.

This is a very simple example, and the strategy is just for illustrating the B PRINCIPLE. Whatever pair of strategies you may adopt for your sales are completely your own and a lot of thought and analysis should go into generating a set of two strategies that will give you a sales advantage. That is on your side, there is no one size fits all, but the value to have here is that there are not one but two strategies that need to be defined and implemented. The core of the B PRINCIPLE.

The B Principle in Human Resources

Once you enter a large company, for example a global company, the head count goes up to thousands, tens of thousands and even hundreds of thousands. In this size and dimensions there is an array of people and job descriptions. Many human resources teams use a categorization and divide the workforce into different job groups or brackets. The salary, compensation and benefits are designed for each group.

When Federico Pareto studied the populations wealth, he found that the wealthy were 20% of the total population. 80% was the middle and lower income. That 20% had 80% of the total wealth of his country, Italy.

In the workforce a good idea is to follow the fact that the correlation found on people's wealth should be a good match for the strategy for the salary and compensation. The idea is to set the top 80% budget salaries in the top 20% job group, the C suite. The rest of the bracket should have the bottom 20% on that total 80%.

If we apply the B PRINCIPLE to the workforce salary and compensation the result should be a compensation package designed specially for the top 20%, the C suite or Directors. Another package should be designed for the remainder of the workforce. A graphical display with the B PRINCIPLE balls diagram displays this case (Diagram 2).

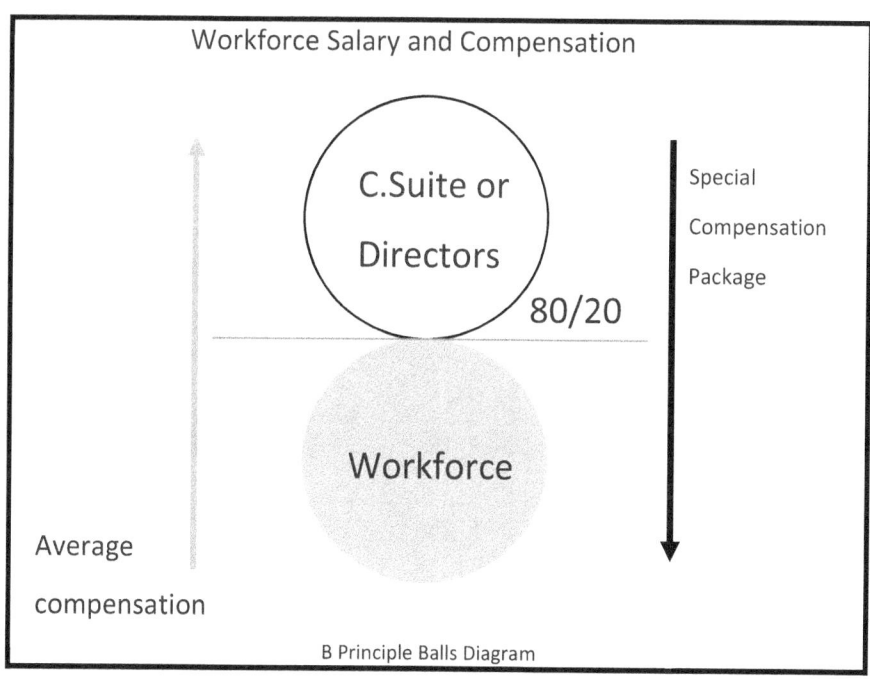

B Principle Balls Diagram

Salary will be defined by job responsibility. As responsibility and accountability goes up so will salary and compensation. That will be the bottom-up approach for the workforce, the bottom 80%. For the top 20% a special compensation package and benefits should be designed accordingly to the high level of responsibility and accountability. This is top talent that runs the company that takes on the hard decisions and steer through adversity. This group develops strategy and seek excellence in execution. You need to attract top talent and retain them with a good healthy benefits pack.

Some may argue that this is not a fair way to compensate the workforce. A more level strategy should be in place. I´m not implying here that this is the only solution, but a mere approach based on best practices in human resources. Not a universal answer but a pretty good one for a realistic approach to business. If your workforce behaves or resembles a Pareto 80/20 proportion, it is the logical way to go. If you keep in mind two things: first that the salary follows a pareto distribution and, second, that whatever strategy you adopt follows the B PRINCIPLE you will have two strategies different in nature that will bring the desired outcome.

The B principle in Life

Life Objectives and priorities

One way to look at your main objectives in life is to set a list and then prioritize them top to bottom on what matters the most. For some it is obvious what to put first; for others they may have no clue and need an intense trip of soul searching. There might be other cases where you think you know those priorities, but your acts are not lined up to those objectives. Whatever is your case there being a Pareto principle present in this objective list. In this case it is not that numerical, but it meets the 80/20 proportion. Your top priorities make up the 20% count of your priorities and the other 80% are less important or non-priorities in your life. Let me explain with my own experience. When I look at what matters in my life and make a list it looks something like this:

1. Family
2. Soul
3. Health
4. Knowledge
5. food
6. friends
7. money
8. music
9. People
10. Climate change

This list is ordered by priorities in my life and the first 3 are the main priorities. Everything I do, the decisions I take all go around the first 3 priorities. For the rest they take time and are taken care of only when the first 3 are what I consider on an OK level. I feel I have a good life and if there is any success to be accounted for it is because I have focused on those main priorities.

The B Principle in this case is setting focus on the top priorities and the second strategy for the bottom ones is to take care of them only when the top is taken care of. If I did not apply the B PRINCIPLE to my life priorities, I probably might be spending too much time and effort on things that matter a whole lot less to me than the main. I will have to spread too thin to cover all and probably fail at one or more top priorities.

Over time this list might change, and a top priority today might be displaced by another in the future or new ones might be added. The idea is to review your list and not lose focus and at the same time cover the rest of priorities. If you only focus on the main priorities, you might lose balance and that is not good either. I've seen this happen with people that focus a lot on one thing like money or work and have other priorities like a loved one that are lost in their sight.

This comes as an example of the B PRINCIPLE outside economics, administration, and business. It also comes as a contribution on my part to a better life that has worked for me. It is both an example and a recommendation. Again, it is not intended to be taken as proven fact but it is based on observation. What I can assure you is that is better than no strategy or strategies at all.

Personal Finance

It is well known that many the average working citizen in the world is under some debt pressure from taking loans and then having trouble repaying them. Some are mortgages, some student loans, car loans and credit card debt. Many come from an unexpected change in income from a lost job or sump in business. Another case is that some people become ill, impaired or unable to generate an income without any warning. There is also the case of just not having enough control over the personal finances. This may be because of lack of financial education or just not being very well organized at all. The word is full of business looking to lure you to spend your money and the attraction can be fatal to your finances. As there are many people with personal finance troubles, there are people that offer their support in the form of personal finance advisors, who have helped a lot of people come out of debt. Usually with some common sense as to sit and give a hard look at the spending habits, their income and develop a strategy. Just from the mere exercise of analysis and a change in habits can get you out of trouble. It is fun to say that I was watching a documentary on personal finance and the support the consultant brought and saw that the B PRINCIPLE was applied. I decided to add this example both to illustrate the B PRINCIPLE and if you have some personal finance improvement maybe take on the advice.

The exercise goes as follows: You make a list of the main spend categories. here is an example:

- Food
- Transportation
- clothes
- eating out and drinks
- rent
- dog food
- insurance
- Energy
- Communications and internet
- health care
- gym

the next step is to add your year spending on this category and dived it into 12 months on the year to get a monthly average:

- Food $300
- Transportation $400
- clothes $200
- eating out and drinks $200
- rent $500
- dog food $100
- insurance $150
- Energy $200
- Communications and internet $100
- health care $100
- gym $65

Then You put the list top down and see where you spend the most:

- rent $500
- Transportation $400
- Food $300
- eating out and drinks $200
- clothes $200
- Energy $200
- insurance $150
- Communications and internet $100

- health care $100
- dog food $100
- gym $65

Total: $2315

The next is to review where the line is drawn in the Pareto Principle of the 80/20:

rent	$ 500.00	22%	22%
Transportation	$ 400.00	17%	39%
Food	$ 300.00	13%	52%
eating out and drinks	$ 200.00	9%	60%
clothes	$ 200.00	9%	69%
Energy	$ 200.00	9%	78%
insurance	$ 150.00	6%	84%
Communications and internet	$ 100.00	4%	89%
health care	$ 100.00	4%	93%
dog food	$ 100.00	4%	97%
gym	$ 65.00	3%	100%
Total	$ 2,315.00		

As you can see the top categories are Rent, Transportation, Food, Eating out and drinks, clothes, Energy. The next step is to develop a savings strategy for each. For Rent it might be to seek a more modest accommodation, for transportation maybe carpooling, food seek less expensive ingredients. for eating out and drinks, maybe limit your outings to less on the week. Energy you can perform the same exercise of listing and then focusing on the main energy spending. This is a case-by-case scenario and how you save is on experience and even creativity. The idea is to use the B PRINCIPLE in defining the strategy for the main categories, in this case focus on them so the lower categories do not distract you. For example, if you go to another gym with a lower subscription say $45 you will be saving $20 instead of focusing on less spend in transport or rent that might reflect $100 or even $200 saved. Hope besides showing a good example on the B PRINCIPLE this exercise gives some food for thought on improving your own personal finances.

The B Principle is a fact

After so many examples where the Pareto Principle applies and then the B principle accompanies it is of my conclusion that whenever you find the pareto principle applied it is a great idea to apply the B principle in developing the strategies for both top 20 and the bottom 80. You can say that the B Principle is the strategy before the developing the strategy pair or as I title this book the strategy before the strategy. It is a piece of knowledge that serves as a strategic approach to developing a strategy for a set of pareto principle occurrences. Hope this will be of value to the reader and will find a guiding light when dealing with strategy development. It took me from not knowing what to do with six hundred plus line items needed to be sourced fast to a winning strategy.

What happened after the accident?

As you may be wondering, the purchasing worked beautifully using the B PRINCIPLE. All the low-cost parts and items we purchased very quickly with one quote since it was low cost. There were a few high-cost items we spent a week or two sourcing and comparing options before we chose a winning offer. All in all, the six hundred plus items got purchased in a very short time and new ones got tended for too. The stakeholders were the plant managers who had a lot of pressure since the power generation plants have very heavy sanctions if they stop unexpectedly. Only programmed maintenance stops are allowed. That said even the smallest, cheapest part can stop the plant. Today I can say proudly that we covered the emergency very well and by developing a dual strategy was key in doing so.

After a couple of months, the injured driver who was going to change jobs was discharged from the hospital. The Human Resources manager convinced the directors to ignore that he had resigned and keep him as if nothing had happened. This way he could stay on board and not lose his job but also the job insurance will help him cover all those months and surgeries in his arm. You might think that he will stay onboard filled with gratitude and be forever thankful to have his medical bill covered and still have a job. Well, it was not the case, he left the company as soon as his medical bills were paid. I really wondered why he was so unappreciative and left anyway. Some six months after the accident I got a piece of information that filled a gap in a puzzle of corruption and deceit.

I had a call from a headhunter for a position in another company again. She said that she knew that I was looking for work since I went to the assessment panel and that there was an opening in this power generation plant that had just opened. No process, no test, no assessment panel, or interviews, just a proposal and it was mine. The salary is just the same as the cement company. It was fishy. I set out to investigate what was going on here. After asking around I found that the girl that was with me on the assessment panel that terrible Saturday was working where the injured driver was going to move. and it was also the company that the headhunter was offering this no questions asked position. Then a friend of mine told me she needed to talk about that assessment panel with the cement company. That was odd since she had nothing to do with that company. So it happened that this guy, one of the panelists in the assessment, was a guy who was hitting on her. He told her about this process and mentioned my name by chance. He told her that it was all rigged and that had him very uneasy. They had a headhunter send them this girl and they decided she was going to be hired no questions asked. But they had to do the assessment panel exercise to comply with contracting policies. They decided to give her in advance a set of questions and answers, tricky questions for her to answer and look good. I almost fell from my chair! I felt a cold rush of blood to my head. No wonder I did so poorly, it was rigged.

I checked who the headhunter was and as you might figure out it was the same that ushered me to the job in the other power plant. She created this scheme where the girls get the job at the cement plant and then I get the one at the other power plant. Why me, simply both the cement plant and the power plant were both clients so she could not take a resource from one and leave them hanging so she filled the void with me. It gets even darker. She will sell the jobs to anyone with the profile that will be paying to be selected. The driver that lost his arm movement used her services to get the new job at the power plant. That closed the circle and explained why after paying for his medicals and keeping him aboard with a job he still left the company. Also, why there was a job still waiting for him after all those months and his disabilities.

I'm still shocked at how everything happened. How corrupt was everything. But at the same time, I'm grateful. Why? Wellbeing at that rigged assessment panel prevented me from being in the accident. I´m a very religious guy and I think God will intervene in all this. I got to skip the accident and had the opportunity to realize such a valuable insight that is the B PRINCIPLE, something that I can pass on to you the reader of this book. It's all good in the end.

and left anyway. Some six months after the accident I got a piece of information that filled a gap in a puzzle of corruption and deceit.

I had a call from a headhunter for a position in another company again. She said that she knew that I was looking for work since I went to the assessment panel and that there was an opening in this power generation plant that had just opened. No process, no test, no assessment panel, or interviews, just a proposal and it was mine. The salary is just the same as the cement company. It was fishy. I set out to investigate what was going on here. After asking around I found that the girl that was with me on the assessment panel that terrible Saturday was working where the injured driver was going to move. and it was also the company that the headhunter was offering this no questions asked position. Then a friend of mine told me she needed to talk about that assessment panel with the cement company. That was odd since she had nothing to do with that company. So it happened that this guy, one of the panelists in the assessment, was a guy who was hitting on her. He told her about this process and mentioned my name by chance. He told her that it was all rigged and that had him very uneasy. They had a headhunter send them this girl and they decided she was going to be hired no questions asked. But they had to do the assessment panel exercise to comply with contracting policies. They decided to give her in advance a set of questions and answers, tricky questions for her to answer and look good. I almost fell from my chair! I felt a cold rush of blood to my head. No wonder I did so poorly, it was rigged.

I checked who the headhunter was and as you might figure out it was the same that ushered me to the job in the other power plant. She created this scheme where the girls get the job at the cement plant and then I get the one at the other power plant. Why me, simply both the cement plant and the power plant were both clients so she could not take a resource from one and leave them hanging so she filled the void with me. It gets even darker. She will sell the jobs to anyone with the profile that will be paying to be selected. The driver that lost his arm movement used her services to get the new job at the power plant. That closed the circle and explained why after paying for his medicals and keeping him aboard with a job he still left the company. Also, why there was a job still waiting for him after all those months and his disabilities.

I'm still shocked at how everything happened. How corrupt was everything. But at the same time, I'm grateful. Why? Wellbeing at that rigged assessment panel prevented me from being in the accident. I´m a very religious guy and I think God will intervene in all this. I got to skip the accident and had the opportunity to realize such a valuable insight that is the B PRINCIPLE, something that I can pass on to you the reader of this book. It's all good in the end.